Teofilo Ernesto Comba

Compendium of Italian pronunciation : (La Pronunzia Italiana); with rules and complete lists of exceptions, alphabetically for ready reference

Teofilo Ernesto Comba

Compendium of Italian pronunciation : (La Pronunzia Italiana); with rules and complete lists of exceptions, alphabetically for ready reference

ISBN/EAN: 9783337157180

Printed in Europe, USA, Canada, Australia, Japan

Cover: Foto ©Paul-Georg Meister /pixelio.de

More available books at **www.hansebooks.com**

COMPENDIUM

OF

ITALIAN PRONUNCIATION

(LA PRONUNZIA ITALIANA).

WITH

RULES AND COMPLETE LISTS OF EXCEPTIONS

TABULATED ALPHABETICALLY FOR READY REFERENCE

BY

T. E. COMBA

AUTHOR OF "LA LINGUA ITALIANA," ETC.

LONDON

HIRSCHFELD BROS.

22-24 BREAMS BUILDINGS

1897

PREFACE.

THE object of this compendium of Italian pronunciation is practical usefulness. It contains rules, lists of exceptions, notes, etc., for which I have frequently been asked.

The arrangement is intended to facilitate ready reference. The tables will be found, I think, sufficiently complete to be serviceable to any student of Italian. As the proper pronunciation of e, o, s, and z really offers serious difficulties, I have thought it advantageous to treat the subject as exhaustively as a work of this character would permit, availing myself of such authorities as Buscaino, Fornari, Moise, Rigutini, and others.

It may be well to state that I am not ignorant of the fact that the same word may be differently pronounced in the various Italian centres. In such cases I have endeavored to be guided by what seem to me the best authorities, inclining, however, I should add, to the Tuscan pronunciation.

I shall be much pleased if this little work prove instrumental in eliminating some of the difficulties which Americans encounter in the study of Italian.

T. E. COMBA.

NEW YORK, *June* 28, 1897.

ITALIAN PRONUNCIATION

(LA PRONUNZIA ITALIANA).

IN Italian the letters are of common gender, and may, therefore, take the masculine or the feminine article before them, with one exception : **K** (cappa) is always masculine.

Following are the letters of the Italian alphabet, with their names in English values. These, of course, can at best only be approximate.

N. B. — *Do not prolong the vowel sounds.*

A, *ah.*	[2] H, *ak'kah.*	O, *o.*	U, *oo.*
B, *be* or *be* [1] (bĕ).	I, *e.*	P, *pe* or *pe* [1].	V, *voo* or *ve* [1].
C, *che* or *che* [1].	J, *e loon'go.*	Q, *coo.*	[3] W, *dop'pio-voo.*
D, *de* or *de* [1].	[3] K, *kap'pah.*	R, *er're* [1].	[3] X, *ik'kasse* [1].
E, *e* [1] (as in *met*).	L, *el'le* [1].	S, *es'se* [1].	[3] Y, *ip'silon.*
F, *ef'fe* [1].	M, *em'me* [1].	T, *te* or *te* [1].	Z, *dze'tah.*
G, *je* or *je* [1].	N, *en'ne* [1].		

[1] E as in *met* (a in *many*, as pronounced by many people) ; or like the *first part* of the sound of **a** in such words as *gate, date, fate;* which, from the Italian standpoint, is really a diphthong equal to **e–i**, a sound which the Italian **e** never has.

[2] H is always silent. With this exception (and the compound consonants **gn** and **sc** which form special combinations), all letters, whether vowels or consonants, must be distinctly sounded.

[3] Strictly speaking, **K, W, X,** and **Y** do not belong to the Italian alphabet. But, inasmuch as they are used in words from foreign languages, it seems proper that they should be known by name.

5

A is pronounced like **a** in *father.* Ex. : *madre,* mother.

B as well as **d, f, l, m, n, p, t,** and **v** are pronounced as in English. There are, it is true, slight shades of difference in **d** and **t,** for instance, but they are almost imperceptible.

Bb like all double consonants, must be pronounced with double emphasis.

C is *hard,* like English **k** :

    1. Before **a, o, u.** Ex. : *cane,* dog ; *cuoco,* cook.

    2. Before any consonant. Ex. : *crudo,* raw ; *chiesa,* church.

    N. B. — **Ch** occurs only before **e** or **i,** and always sounds like **k.**

C is *soft,* like **ch** in *chest,* before **e** or **i.** Ex. : *cencio,* rag ; *ciocca,* tuft ; *ciancia,* idle talk.

    N. B. — **Sc** before **e** or **i** is equal to **sh** in *ship.* Ex.: *scettro,* sceptre.

Cc before **a, o, u,** or *a consonant,* has the sound of English **k,** with double emphasis. Ex. : *ecco,* behold.

    Before **e** or **i, cc** is pronounced like **tch** in *etching,* always with a double emphasis. Ex. : *faccia,* face ; *feccia,* dregs ; *freccia,* arrow.

D is pronounced as in English. **Dd** with double emphasis.

E has two sounds, one *close,* the other *open* or *broad.*

    E *close* is like **e** in *met* (or **a** in *many*). Ex.: *me ne vo,* I go away.

    E *open* is like **a** in *mare.* Ex. : *merito,* merit.

As it is very difficult for foreigners, and not always easy for Italians, to know when the **e** (and the **o**) is *close* and when it is *open,* it was thought best to offer the following notes in a tabulated form.

Unaccented e is always close.

Generally speaking, when accented e is derived from the Latin ĭ or ē, e *is close.* Ex.: *capello,* from capillus; *godere,* from gaudere. And when from the Latin ĕ or æ, e *is open.* Ex. : *servo,* from servus ; *premio* from premium. There are but few exceptions to this rule.

E is CLOSE.	E is OPEN.
Rule:	*Exceptions:*
In *monosyllables* and *last syllables accented.*	1. *è* (is), *eh ! se'* (thou art), *c'è* (there is), *te'* (for *tieni,* hold), *me'* (*meglio,* better), *re* (musical note), *che!* (nonsense !), *cioè, coccodè, bembè,* (ben bene), and the interjections *ahimè, ohimè, immè, madiè.*
Ex. : e, se, sè, ce, te, me, re, che, tre, ne ; perchè, chè, poichè, testè, rendè, credè, vendè.	

2. Proper names : *Mosè, Noè, Giosuè, Siloè.*
3. Nouns of foreign origin : *Caffè, canapè, aloè, tè* or *thè, lacchè,* etc.

Exceptions:		*Rule:*
1. In *Imperfects.* Ex.: credea, temea, etc.	**Ea,** **Eo,**	Followed by another *vowel.*
2. In *Preterites.* Ex.: credei, temei, etc., and credeo, feo, temeo, etc. (for credè, fè, temè, etc.).	**Ei.**	Ex. : reo, neo, assemblea, platea, dea (goddess), Maccabei, Ebreo, Reuma, neutro, Nereidi, idea, miei, dei (thou must, or, the gods).

3. Also in *quei, ei, ehi,* and *dei, pei, nei* (art. prep.), *bea* (beva), *stea* (stia), *fea* (faceva), *dea* (dia, let him give).

8 ITALIAN PRONUNCIATION.

E is CLOSE.		E is OPEN.

Exceptions:

1. All diminutive nouns in *ietto*.
   Ex.: maschietto, fischietto, malizietta, etc.
2. Abstract nouns in *iezza*.
   Ex. : vecchiezza, saviezza, etc.

Ie.

Rule:
Preceded by i expressed or suppressed.
   Ex.: cielo, siepe, siete, piede, diede, cieco; ingegnere (ingeniere), altero (altiero), breve (brieve), etc.

3. Also, *Bietta.* — *Chierico.* — *Glielo.* — *Intiero* (from intĕger). — *Schietto, siegue.* — *Tregua.*

Exceptions:

Bebbi (bevvi) and similar forms. — *Crebbe.* — *Debito* (n. and adj.). — *Increbbe.* — *Lebbra.* — *Nebbia.* — *Rebbio.* *Strebbio.* — *Trebbio, Trebbia* (proper n.).

Eb.

Rule:
Followed by **b, bb,** or **b** *and another consonant.*
   Ex. : Febo, plebe ; ebbe, farebbe ; ebbro, palpebre.

Exceptions:

Meco, teco, seco (con me, etc.). All forms of the verb *secare*, to saw, to cut. As: *io seco, tu sechi, egli seca*, etc.

Eca, Eche, Echi, Eco, Ecu ; Ecl, Ecn.

Rule:
Followed by c hard.
   Ex.: arreco, arrechi, arreca, pecora, secolo, eco, Tecla, tecnico.

E is CLOSE.		E is OPEN.

Rules:		*Exceptions:*
1. Followed by **cc** *hard.*	**Ecc;**	*Bernecche.* — *Cecia.* — *Deci-*
Ex.: stecca, secchio, orec-	**Ecc,**	*mo, decima* (n. and v.), *dieci.*
chia, becco, etc.	**Eci.**	— *Eccito, ecco.* — *Fece* (n.),
2. Followed by **c** or **cc** *soft.*		*feccia.* — *Mecca* (varnish). —
Ex.: fece, feci ; freccia,		*Pecca* (n. and v.), *pecchero,*
frecce.		*pecciolo, pernecche, prece.* —

Recere, recipe, recita (n. and v.). — *Salamelecche, schimbescio, sottecche, specchio* (n. and v.), *specie.* — *Vecchio.*

Proper Names : *Abimelecco, Decio, Grecia, Giudecca, Mecca, Rebecca,* etc.

Exceptions:		*Rule:*
Credere (comp. and verbal	**Ed.**	Followed by **d** or **dd**.
forms), *credito, cedro.* —		Ex.: Sedia, cedola, incre-
Edera. — *Fede, freddo* (adj.,		dulo.
n., and v.). — *Mercede.* —		

Poledro. — *Sedici.* — *Tredici.* — *Vedo* (and other forms).

Proper Names : *Alfredo, Goffredo, Manfredo, Toledo,* etc.

Exceptions:		*Rule:*
Artefice. — *Carnefice.* — *In-*	**Ef.**	Followed by **f** or **ff**.
trefolo. — *Orefice, ortefica.*		Ex. : acefalo, benefico ;
— *Partefice, pontefice.* —		effe, beffa (n. and v.).
Refe. — *Stefano, strefolo.* —		
Trefolo.		

E is CLOSE.		**E is OPEN.**
Rules:		*Exceptions:*
1. Followed by *hard* **g** or **gg.**	**Eg,**	*Aggrego, annego, apotegma.*
Ex.: Lega, segolo, segue,	**Egg,**	— *Bega.* — *Chieggo, chieg-*
stregghia, traveggo, etc.	**Egf,**	*gia, collega* (n.), *contegno*
2. Followed by *soft* **gg** or **g**	**Egl,**	(v.), *convegno* (v.), *congrega*
before another consonant.	etc.	(n. and v.). — *Disgrego.* —
Ex.: Legge (n.), solfeggio,		*Egloga, egro.* — *Impiego* (n.
egli, contegno (n.), degno,		and v.). — *Meglio.* — *Niego*
sostegno (n.), negro, etc.		(n. and v.). — *Omega.* —
		Pareglio, peggio, piega (n.

and v.), *prego* (n. and v.). — *Regola* (n. and v.), *regolo, reggia.* —
Seggia, seggio, seggiola, seggo, sostegno (v.), *speglio, spegno.* —
Tegno. — *Ritegno* (v.). — *Vegeto* (v. and adj.), *veglio* (for vec-
chio), *vegno* (and deriv.).

Different forms of verbs in **eggere,** like *seggo, posseggo, protegge,*
reggo, leggo, chieggio, etc.

Proper Names, like *Diego, Egla, Flegra, Orneglia, Regolo, Reggio*
(d'Emilia).

N. B. — *Reggio di Calabria* is given the close sound of **e** by the
Southerners.

Exceptions:		*Rule:*
Dilegine. — *Fregio* (n. and v.). — *Solegina.*	**Egi.**	Followed by *soft* **g.** Ex.: *collegio, Norvegia,* etc.
Exception:		*Rule:*
Capistejo.	**Ej.**	Followed by **j.** Ex.: Plejadi, epopeja, etc.

E is CLOSE		E is OPEN.
Exceptions:		*Rule:*
Ancella, attelo. — *Belva.* —	**EI,**	Followed by **l** or **ll.**
Candela, capello.—*Del, del-*	**Ell.**	Ex.: Cappello, fratello;
la, dello. — *Elba, elce, ella,*		elice, Vangelo, Adele, etc.
ello, elleno, ellera, elmo. —		
Fedele (pr. n.), *felce, felpa,*		

feltro. — *Glielo.* — *Melma, mela* (n. and v.), *melo.* — *Nel, nella,* *nello.* — *Pelo* (n. and v.), *pel* (art. prep.). — *Quello.* — *Ragnatelo.* — *Scandella, scelgo, scelse, scelta, scelto, selce, Sele, selva, selice,* *stella.* — *Tela, telo* (piece of cloth), *tordela, trapelo* (n. and v.). — *Vela, velo* (n. and v.).

Exceptions:		*Rules:*
Blasfema. — *Femina.* — *Ma-*	**Em,**	1. Followed by **m** *single.*
remma, memma. — *Prezze-*	**Emm.**	Ex.: Poema, premio, ge-
molo.—*Scemo* (adj. and v.),		mito, tema (theme), etc.
semina (n. and v.), *seme, se-*		2. Followed by **mm**, in words
mola. — *Tema* (fear; n. and		accented on the penulti-
v.).		mate.
Futures in **emo.**		Ex.: Gemma, stemma, di-
Ex.: faremo, diremo, etc.		lemma, etc.
Conditionals in **emmo.**		

Ex.: faremmo, etc.

Preterites in **emmo.**

Ex.: facemmo, etc.

Antiquated forms of *Pres. Ind.* in **emo.**

Ex.: semo, avemo, etc.

E is **CLOSE**.		E is **OPEN**.

Rules:

1. Followed by **m** and another consonant.
   Ex. : Nembo, lembo, scempio (n., adj., and v.), semplice, etc.
2. Followed by **mm**, in words accented on the antepenult.
   Ex. : Bestemmia, vendemmia, etc.

Emb,
etc.
Emm.

Exceptions:

Contemplo. — *Esempio.* — *Flemmone.* — *Grembo.* — *Lemmo.* — *Membro.* — *Sempre.* — *Tempia, tempio, tempo, tempera* or *tempra* (n. and v.).
Names of the months : *Settembre, novembre, dicembre.*

Exceptions:

Addormento, alena (n. and v.), *allena, altalena, altaleno, arcobaleno, arena* (sand), *avena, ascendere, appena.* — *Balena* (n. and v.), *baleno.* — *Catena, cena* (v. and n.), *cenere.* — *Divento, dimentico* (adj. and v.), *domenica.* — *Entro* (prep. and v.), *endice.*

En,
Enc,
Enn.

Rules:

1. Followed by **n** *single* or **n** *before another consonant.*
   Ex. : Scena, bene, mensa, sento, etc.
2. Followed by **nn,** in words accented on the antepenult.
   Ex. : Rendita, Agamennone, etc.

— *Falena, freno* (n. and v.). — *Gliene.* — *Lena, lendine.* — *Maddalena, mena* (n. and v.), *meno, menimo, mento* (n.), *mendico, mentre, mentovo.* — *Pena* (n. and v.), *pergamena, pentola, pentolo.* — *Rammendo* (n. and v.), *reni* (le). — *Safena, seno, senza, sereno, scendere, senici, sbrendolo.* — *Terreno, trenta, Trento.* — *Veleno, vena, venti* (20), *vendere* (and deriv.), *vendico.* — *Zeuzero.*

| E is CLOSE. | E is OPEN. |

Exceptions (*continued*):

Words in which **n** is followed by soft **c** or **f**, as: *Prence, enfio, cencio* (except *Cencio* for *Vincenzo, Nencia* for *Lorenza*, and *Menfi*).
Nouns (not adj. and part.) in **mento, menta, mente.**
    Ex.: Nutrimento, etc.
Verbs derived from such nouns. Ex.: Lamenta (from lamento), etc.
Adverbs in **mente.** Ex.: Rettamente, etc.

Rule:		*Exceptions:*
Followed by **nn**, in words accented on the penultimate. Ex.: Penna, venne, ottenni, senno, etc.	**Enn.**	*Ammenne, andrienne.—Benna, bienne* (and the other comp. of *anno*), *bipenne. — Denno* (devono), *dienno* (diedero). *— Enne* (N), *enno* (sono). *— Geenna. — Indenne. — Perenne. — Solenne.*

Proper Names: *Ardenne, Brenno, Cajenna, Enna* (village), *Gebenna, Gujenna, Lenno, Perpenna, Porsenna*, etc.

Exceptions:		*Rule:*
Atrepice. — Discepolo. — Ginepro. — Molteplice. — Pepe.	**Ep,** **Epl,** **etc.**	Followed by **p** single or **p** before a consonant. Ex.: Epa, tepido, peplo, lepre, etc.

Rule:		*Exceptions:*
Followed by **pp.** Ex.: Ceppo, greppia, etc.	**Epp.**	*Seppi* (from *sapere*). Proper Names: *Aleppo, Beppe, Dieppe, Giuseppe.*

	E is CLOSE.		**E is OPEN.**

| | **Eq.** | *Rule:*
Followed by **q.** |

Ex. : Esequie, ossequio, requie, requia (v.).

Exceptions:		**Er,** **Err.**	*Rule:*
Cera (bees-wax), *cerca* (n.			Followed by **r** or **rr.**
and v.), *cercine, cerchio* (n.			Ex. : Primavera, querulo,
and v.), *cherico, chierico, ci-*			erpice, ferro, etc.
cerchia, cuterzola. — *Ermo,*			

erta, erto. — *Fero* (fecero), *ferma* (n. and v.), *fermo.* — *Intero,*
intiero. — *Lercio.* — *Nero, nerola.* — *Pero* and *pera* (n.), *per,*
palischermo, podere. — *Rinvergo.* — *Scerre* (scegliere), *scherma,*
schermo, scherno, scherzo (n. and v.), *sera, serqua, sverza.* — *Verde,*
verga (n. and v.), *vergine, vergola, vero, verzica.*
Infinitives in **ére**, like *sedere, vedere,* etc.
Third pers. pl. of Preterites in **erono**, as : *poterono,* etc.

Rules:		*Exceptions:*
1. Followed by **s** before a	**Es,**	*Bleso.* — *Chiesa, chiesi, cri-*
vowel in words accented on	**Esc,**	*menlese, catacresi, catechesi.*
the penultimate.	**Esp.**	— *Despota.* — *E s e g e s i,*
Ex.: Contesa, francese, sor-		*espero, esco, esca* (n. and v.).
preso, etc.		— *Leso, lesi.* — *Nespolo, ne-*
2. Followed by **sc** *hard* or **sp,**		*spola.* — *Obeso.* — *P e s c o,*
even in words accented on		*pesca* (tree, fruit, and a
the penultimate.		bruise). — *Teschio, tesi* (n.).
Ex. : Vescovo, fresco, ce-		— *Vespa, vespero* or *vespro.*
spite, etc.		Proper Names: *Agnesi, Cre-*
		so, Lachesi, Teresa, etc.

E is CLOSE.		E is OPEN.

E is CLOSE.

Exceptions:

Bestia, bracchese, Brescia. — *Cesare, cesta, cesto* (plant, and for *cesta*), *cestola, capestro, cotesto, cresta, crescere.* — *Desto* (adj. and v.). — *Esso.* — *Fesso* (n. and v.). — *Increscere.* — *Lesso, lesina* (n. and v.). — *Mescere, mescita, messa* (n. and v.), *mestica* (n. and v.), *mesto*

Ess,	
Esc,	
etc.	
Es.	

E is OPEN.

Rules:

1. Followed by ss or s before another consonant.
    Ex.: Cipresso, tessere, estasi, presto, testo, testa, etc.
2. Followed by s before a vowel in words accented on the antepenult.
    Ex. : Fiesole, esito, centesimo, etc.

(adj. and v.), *mestola, mestolo, medesimo.* — *Pesce, pesca* (n. and v., from *pescare*), *pesta* (n., adj., and v.), *Pescia, pesolo.* — *Quaresima, questo.* — *Sghescia, spesso, stesso, svescia.* — *Vescia.*

Nouns in **esimo :** Cristianesimo, paganesimo, etc.

Deriv. of **mettere :** Permesso, commesso, etc.

Verbal endings in Preterites, and Imp. Subj. in **esti, este ; essi, esse, essero,** as : Avesti, aveste ; facessi, facesse, facessero, etc.

Second p. s. of Condit. Pres. in **esti :** Temeresti, etc.

Feminine nouns in **essa :** Principessa, poetessa, ostessa, leonessa, etc.

Rules:

1. Followed by **tt** in diminutives.

Ett.	*No Exception.*

Ex. : Giovinetto, libretto, amaretto, etc.

Also in : *Accetta* (n.). — *Bajonetta, belletta, bietta, biglietto.* —

E is CLOSE.	E is OPEN.

Civetta. — *Detto* (with all comp. from *dire,* like *disdetta, contraddetto,* etc.). — *Fazzoletto, fetta, fretta.* — *Ghetto.* — *Metto* (with all comp. from *mettere,* as *commetto, ammetto,* etc.). — *Netto.* — *Picchetto, pretto.* — *Saetta, salvietta, soffietto, sonetto, sorbetto, stretto* (with all comp. from *stringere,* as *costretto, distretto,* etc.). *Tetto.* — *Vendetta, vetta.* — *Zibetto.*

2. All forms of verbs in **ettare,** derived from a diminutive, or from words in the above list : as, *io umetto* (from *umettare,* from *umidetto*), *io svetto* (from *svettare,* from *vetta*), etc. ; and so the forms of the verbs *balbettare, calettare, cinguettare, dettare, traghettare.*

Exceptions:

Abete, aceto. — *Bettola, brettine, Busseto.* — *Cheto* (adj. and v.), *cometa, creta, cutrettola.* — *Decreto, diavoleto, discreto, diletico* (n. and v.). — *Farchetola.* — *Gaeta, greto, gretola.* — *Inseto.* — *Letico, librettine.* — *Meta* (dung), *minareto, moneta, mettere* (with comp. and deriv.). — *Parete, parletico, pianeta, peto* (n. and v.). — *Rete.* — *Sangioveto* (grape), *segreto,*

Ett, Et, Etn, etc.

Rules:

1. Followed by **tt** in words other than diminutives, (all verbal endings in **etti, ette, ettero**), and those accented on the antepenult.

Ex. : Credetti, credettero, accetto, oggetto, protetto, diletto, cospetto, etc.

2. Followed by **t** single, or before a consonant.

Ex. : Dieta, eretico, poetico, retina, Etna, etc.

---

seta, sete (n.). *setola, sgretolo, solletico, Spoleto.* — *Tappeto, trettica.* — *Vetro, vetrice.*

E is CLOSE.	E is OPEN.

Collective nouns in **eto, eta** : as, pineta, oliveto, etc.

Presents, Futures, and Imperatives in **ete** : as, avete, farete, temete, etc.

Rule:		*Exceptions:*
Followed by **v** or **vv**. Ex. : Neve, beva, bevve, bisognevole, etc.	**Ev, Evv.**	*Allevio* (v.).—*Benevolo, breve* and deriv.).—*Devo, devono, deve, devi.* — *Evito, evo.* — *Greve.* — *Leva* (n. and v.),

longevo. — *Malevolo.* — *Parasceve, persevero, previo.* — *Sevo.*

Proper Names : *Eva, Levi, Mevio, Scevola, Treveri,* etc., etc.

	Ez.	*Rule:* Followed by **z** single. Ex. : Venezia, Lucrezia, facezia, inezia, etc.

Rule:		*Exceptions:*
Followed by **zz**. Ex. : Bellezza, fermezza, brezza, mezzo (over ripe), etc.	**Ezz.**	*Mezzo* (half, middle). — *Pezzo, pezza, prezzo,* and deriv.: as, *appezza, spezzo, apprezza, disprezzo.*

F is pronounced as in English. **Ff** with double emphasis.

G is *hard*, like English **k** :

    1. Before **a, o, u.** Ex. : *gatto,* cat; *goffo,* stupid ; *guida,* guide.

    2. Before any consonant except **li** and **n.** Ex. : *grido,* cry ;

conglomerare, to conglomerate; *inglese,* English; *ghiaccio,* ice; *mughetto,* lily of the valley.

N. B. — **Gh** only occurs before **e** or **i**.

G is *soft,* like **g** in *gentleman,* before **e** or **i**. Ex.; *gente,* people; *Giorgio,* George.

Gg is hard, like English **k,** wherever **g** would be hard, and must be pronounced with double emphasis. Ex.: *raggomitolare,* to wrap up; *ragguaglio,* report, notice; *agghiaccio,* sheep-cote; *agghermigliare,* to clasp.

Before **e** or **i** **gg** is *soft,* and pronounced like **dg** in *edging.* Ex.: *oggi,* to-day; *distrugge,* he destroys.

Gll is pronounced like **lll** in *brilliant.* Ex.: *briglia,* bridle : *cordoglio,* affliction.

Exceptions:

Negligere and its deriv., *negligente, negligenza,* etc. *Gliconio, Angli, Anglicano, Anglia, geroglifo, glicerina,* and a very few more words from the Greek and other foreign languages.

Gn is pronounced like **nl** in *union.* Ex.: *ugna,* finger-nail; *ognuno,* every one; *agnello,* lamb.

H is never pronounced. Ex.: *ho,* I have, is pronounced **o**. It is used as a graphic sign, to harden the **c** and **g** before **e** and **i**. Ex.: *Duchessa,* duchess; *fichi,* figs; *streghe,* witches; *funghi,* mushrooms. **Hh** never occurs.

I is pronounced like **e** in *me.* Ex.: *mio,* my; *confini,* boundaries. N. B. — **I** is sometimes used for euphony in such words as *istrada* (strada), road; *istudio* (studio), study; *tiene,* he holds; *siedo,* I sit; and in verbal forms, — *cambii,* thou changest, etc., in which case the **i** is very short.

J is pronounced like **i**, of which it often takes the place between two vowels. Ex. ; *gioja*, joy.

V. Remarks on the use of the **J**, at page 44.

K is pronounced as in the language from which it may be borrowed.

L as in English. **Ll** with double emphasis.

M as in English. **Mm** with double emphasis.

N as in English. **Nn** with double emphasis.

N. B. — The nasal sound of English **ng** is heard when **n** comes before **c, g** *hard*, and **q**. Ex. : *stanco*, tired ; *stanga*, window-bar ; *dunque*, then.

O has *two* sounds, one *close*, the other *open* or *broad*.

O *close* is like **o** in *pope*. Ex. : *potere*, to be able.

O *open* is like **o** in *for*. Ex. : *forte*, strong.

As it is difficult in many cases to know whether **o** is close or open, the study of the following tables will be found very helpful.

Unaccented **o** is always close.

When **o** comes from the Latin **ō** or **ŭ**, it is *close*.

Ex. : *Ordine*, from *ordo ;* *ove*, from *ubi*.

When **o** comes from the Latin **ŏ** or **au**, it is *open*.

Ex. : *Morte*, from *mors ;* *oro*, from *aurum*.

Exception: coda, tail ; **o** *close*.

O is CLOSE.	O is OPEN.
Exceptions:	*Rules:*
1. *Lo, o, oh! con, co'* (coi), *co* (capo), *sciò!* (shoo !).	1. In monosyllables and *parole tronche;* i. e., words accented on the last vowel.
2. *Coda* (from *cauda*).	

Ex.: Po, do, fo, and ò, però, ho.

2. When **o** stands for **au**.

Ex.: Oro (auro), lode (laude), tesoro (tesauro), etc.

Exceptions:		*Rule:*
1. *Coi* (con i), *noi, voi.*	**Oa, Oe, Oi, etc.**	When followed by a vowel.
2. In the verbal forms *ingoi, impastoi, spastoi, ingoino, impastoino, spastoino;* from *ingojare, impastojare, spastojare.*		Ex.: Stoa, eroe, Zoe, poi, puoi, vuoi, etc.

Exceptions:		*Rule:*
Ottobre. — Robbia.	**Ob.**	When followed by **b** or **bb**.
Forms of the verb *conoscere;* i. e., *conobbi, conobbe,* etc.		Ex.: Robe, gobba, obbrobrio, etc.

Exceptions:		*Rule:*
Atroce. — Bocca, bocchi. — Cioccia (n. and v.), *conocchia, croce. — Doccia, doccio* (n. and v.). *— Feroce, foce. — Goccia* and *gocciola* (n. and v.). *— Moccio, moccico, m o c c o l.o. — Noce* (n.). *—*	**Oc.**	When followed by **c** or **cc**.
		Ex.: Boccia, oca, rocca (f o r t r e s s), ipocrita, mediocre, suocero, carroccio, tocca (cloth), tocco (cap, piece), etc.

Poccia (n. and v.) *— Rocca* (distaff). *— Tocca* (a hole), *tocca* and *tocco* (from *toccare* and for one o'clock). *— Veloce, voce, vocia.*

O is CLOSE.		O is OPEN.
Exceptions: *Coda, code, codola, codolo.* — *Dodici.* — *Rodere* with its compounds and derivatives.	**Od.**	*Rule:* When followed by **d**. Ex.: Frode, lode, lodo, modo, moda, fodera, etc.
Exceptions: *Battisoffia.* — *Cosoffiola.* — *Soffice, soffio* (n. and v. with deriv.).	**Of.**	*Rule:* When followed by **f** or **ff**. Ex.: Goffo, sofo, soffre, orfanotrofio, etc.
Exceptions: *Affogo.* — *Boga, boglio, bogli- olo, borboglia.* — *Cogli* (con gli). — *Doga.* — *Foga* (n. and v.). — *Germoglio* (n.	**Og.**	*Rule:* When followed by **g** or **gg**. Ex.: Toga, pioggia, elo- gio, rogito, togliere, etc.

and v.), *giogo, gorgoglio* (n. and v.). — *Logoro* (n., adj., and v.). —
Moglie. — *Orgoglio.* — *Rigoglio, roggio, rogo* (*rovo*, briar). — *Soga.*
— *Voga.*

Rule: When followed by **gn**. Ex.: Menzogna, bisogno, agogna (v.), etc.	**Ogn.**	*Exceptions:* *Agogna* (river). — *Bologna.* — *Cognito, cogno* (conio), *Cologna.* — *Incognito.* — *Progne.* — *Togno* (Tonio).
Rule: When followed by **j**. Ex.: Feritoja, cesoje, fila- tojo, lavatoj, rasoj, etc.	**Oj.**	*Exceptions:* *Ancroja.* — *Boja, Boi* (n. pl.). — *Convojo* (n. and v.), *cuojo,* *crojo.* — *Dimojo.* — *Gioja.* — *Leucojo, loja, lojola.* — *Moje,*

O is CLOSE.   **O is OPEN.**

Exceptions (*continued*) :

moja, muojo. — *Noja* (n. and v.). — *Precojo* or *procojo.* — *Ribuoja.* — *Soja, salamoja, Savoja, squarquojo, stuoja.* — *Troja* (pr. and c. n.).

Exceptions:	0l.	*Rule:*
Ampolla, ascolto (n. and v.). — *Biroldo, bolla* and *bollo* (n. and v. from *bollare* and *bollire*), *bolgia, bolso, brollo* (brullo). — *Catollo, cipolla,*		1. When followed by **l** or **ll.** Ex. : Scuola, nolo, colgo, soldo, colla (n.), collo (n.), etc.

cocolla, corolla, corollo, col, collo (con lo), *colla* (con la), *cola* and *colo* (n. and v. from *colare*), *colto* (adj. and n.), *consolo.* — *Folgore, folta* (n. and adj.). — *Gola.* — *Ingolla* and *ingollo* (n. and v.). — *Lolla.* — *Manigoldo, midolla, midollo, molto.* — *Polla, pollo, polso, polvere.* — *Rampollo* (n. and v.), *ruspollo.* — *Satollo* (n., adj., and v.), *scapolla, scolo* (n. and v.), *scolta, sepolto, soggolo, sole, solo, sollo* (adj.), *spolvero* (n. and v.), *stollo, stolto.* — *Volo* (n. and v.), *volgo* (n.), *volto* (n.), *volva.*

Rule 2:	0l	*Exceptions to 2:*
When **l** is followed by **c, f, m, p, t**: as, Dolce, solco, golfo, zolfo, olmo, coltre, colpa, volto, etc.		*Colchico* (n. and adj.), *colco* (v.), *solfa* (mus. term), *colto* (from *cogliere*), *sciolto* (from *sciogliere*), *volto* (from *volgere*).

Proper Names : *Colco, Colchide, Stocolma, Astolfo, Marcolfo,* and others in **olfo.**

O is CLOSE.	**O is OPEN.**
Exceptions:	*Rule:*
Cocomero, come. — Domo (v. and adj.). — Gomena, gomito. — Lome (lume). — Nome (n.). — Pomo, pomice. — **Om.**	When followed by **m** simple. Ex. : Comodo, uomo, Como, nomina, etc.

Romice. — Toma and tomo (from tomare, n. and v.).
Proper Names : Roma, Romolo.

Rule:		*Exceptions:*
When followed by **mm,** or **m** and another consonant. Ex. : Gomma, somma, rombo, piombo, etc.	**Omb, Omm, etc.**	Comma, commodo (n., v., and deriv.), complice, compito.— Domma (dogma).

Rules:		*Exceptions:*
1. When followed by **n** simple in monosyllables and words accented on the penultimate (*parole piane*). Ex.: Padrone, c o r o n a, sono (I am, they are), con, non, etc. 2. When followed by **n** and another consonant (*s impura*). Ex.: Onda, trionfo, pronto, gonfio, etc. Also: *Alfonso, Ildefonso.*	**On, Ond, Onf, Ong, Ongr, Ons, etc.**	A. Buono. — Dittongo (also trittongo, quadrittongo). — Colono, concavo, condito, conjuge, cono. — Frastuono. — Giona. — Incondito, ipocondrio. — Nona (n. and adj.). — Patrono, polono, ponce, pondero, pondo, pontico, prono. — Onere. — Recondito. — Suono (n. and v.), spondulo. — Testimone, tono, trono, tuono. — Zona. B. When **n** is followed by **s,** or by another consonant, in

words accented on the antepenult.

O is **CLOSE.**   O is **OPEN.**

Exceptions (*continued*)

Ex.: Intonso, console, responso, congruo, congrega, etc.

C. Adj. in **ontico :** as Anacreontico, acherontico, etc.

D. Proper Names : *Ascalona, Bajona, Epaminonda, Ponto, Ponzio,* etc. Except : *Alfonso* and *Ildefonso.*

Exceptions:		*Rules:*
Cionno, colonna. — *Garonna.* — *O n i c e.* — *S o n n o.* — *Tonno.*	**On,** **Onn.**	1. When followed by **n** simple, in words accented on the antepenult. Ex.: Antonio, Aonio, intonaco, monaca, etc. 2. When followed by **nn.** Ex.: Donna, eleisonne, gonna, amonno (amarono), etc.
Exceptions:		*Rule:*
Dopo, doppio and *doppia* (n., adj., and v.). — *Coppo.* — *Groppo.* — *Poppa* (n. and v.). — *Scopa, sopra, stoppa* (n. and v.), *stoppia, stroppa* or *stroppia.*	**Op,** **Opp.**	When followed by **p** or **pp.** Ex.: Topo, coppa, intoppo, copia, coppia, popolo, opera, etc.
	Oq.	*Rule:* When followed by **q.** Ex.: Celoquio, colloquio, etc.

O is CLOSE.

Rules:

1. When followed by **r** single in words accented on the penultimate, and especially in nouns and adjectives in **ore** and their fem. **ora.**

   Ex.: Fiore, ora, ancora, signore, filatora, imperatore, candore, foro, etc.
2. When followed by **rr.**

   Ex.: Torre (n.), borro, correre, borra, etc.

**Or,
Orr.**

O is Open.

Exceptions:

Aborro, alloro, Azzorre. — *Barbassoro, battiloro.*—*Cantimplora, cuore* or *core* (and the like, as *crepacuore, accora,* etc.), *coro, canoro, camorra, camorro, castoro, ciporro, correo, corre* (cogliere). — *Decoro* (n. and v.), *dimora* (n. and v.), *Dora* (pr. n. and v.). — *Fora* (sarebbe), *fuori, fuore, fuora* (as also *fora,* etc.), *foro* (a place). — *Gora,* *granciporro.* — *Moro* (n.), *moro* (v. and adj.). — *Naborre, nasorre, nuora* or *nora.* — *Ora* (aura), *oro, orrido.* — *Poro, porro, pretorio, prora.* — *Risporo, ritorre* (ritogliere). — *Suora, sora* (v.), *sciorre* (sciogliere), *stajoro, sonoro.* — *Tesoro, toro, torre* (togliere), *torrido.*

Proper Names : *Teodoro, Gomorra, Flora, Antenora,* etc.

Forms of the verbs : *Dimorare, decorare, deflorare, deplorare, dorare, esplorare, ignorare, implorare, imporrare, intorare, irrorare, morire, orare, plorare, ristorare,* and words formed with *core.*

O is CLOSE.		O is OPEN.

<table>
<tr><td>

Exceptions:

Accorcio (n. and v.), *accorse* (from *correre*), *adorno* (adj. and v.), *aggiorno* (n.). — *Balordo, bagordo, borsa, borgo, bitorzolo, borbora* (*burbera*), *bornia.* — *Corte* (n.), *corto, capitorzolo, corsa* (from *correre*, also other forms). — *Disordine.* — *Forca, forcola, forcolo, forfora, forma* (n. and v.), *forno, forse, fra-*

</td><td>

Or,
Orb,
Orc,
Ord,
Orp,
Ors,
Ort,
etc.

</td><td>

Rules:

1. When followed by **r** simple in words accented on the antepenult.
    Ex.: Boria, florido, storico, storia, dorico, flora, etc.
2. When followed by **r** before another consonant.
    Ex.: Morbo, corda, corpo, morto, forte, Corso, torse, etc.

</td></tr>
</table>

storno. — *Giorgio, gorbia, gorgo, giorno.* — *Ingordo, ingorgo, imborgo* (v.), *imporpora, inforco,* (v.), *informo, intorno.* — *Livorno, lordo* (adj. and v.). — *Mormore.* — *Organo, orcio, ordine, ordina* (v.), *orno* (n. and v.), *orlo* (n. and v.), *orma, orso, Orsola.* — *Porpora, ponte, porla* (porre la). — *Quattordici.* — *Ricorso, riforma, risorto* (and every form of risorgere), *rimborso* (n.). — *Sborso* (v.), *scorcio* (n. and v.), *scortico, scorso* (scorcio), *sgorbia* (n.), *sgorga* (v.), *sorcio, sorcolo, sordo, sorgere* (and deriv. *sorgo,* etc.), *sorso, stormo, storno.* — *Torba* (n., adj., and v.), *torbido, tordo, torma, tornio* and *torno* (n., v., and adv.), *torso, torsolo, torta* (food), *tortora* or *tortola.*

O is CLOSE.		**O is OPEN.**
Rule:		*Exceptions:*
When followed by s simple in words accented on the penultimate.	Os.	*Arrose* (from *arrogere*). — *Basoso, Beroso.* — *Chiosa* or *glosa* (n. and v.), *cosa, coso.*
Ex.: Annosa, rosa (from rodere), posi, rispose, vizioso, etc.		—*Dosa* (n. and v.), *dose.* — *Esoso.* — *Oso* (v. and adj.). — *Posa* (n. and v.), *prosa.* — *Riposo* (n. and v.), *rosa*

(flower), *roso* (rosajo). — *Sposa.* — *Uosa.*
Greek nouns ending in *osi,* as, *Metempsicosi, ipotiposi, apoteosi,* etc.

Exceptions:		*Rules:*
Agosto. — *Bosso.*— *Conoscere* (and deriv.). — *Fosco.* — *Mosca, moscio, mostra* (n. and v.), *mosto, mostro.* — *Prevosto.* — *Rosso, rossola, rossolo.* — *Tosco* (Tuscan) *tosse.*	Oss, Osd, etc.	1. When followed by ss or s before another consonant. Ex.: Fossa, arrosto, oste, costa, ossa, tossico; imposta (shutter), posta (P.O. and der.), imposto (I mail), apposta (from appostare), etc.
The forms of the verb *essere,* like *fossi, fosti,* etc. Derivatives of *nascondere, rispondere, porre,* as *nascosto, risposto,* etc.		2. When followed by s single in words accented on the antepenult. Ex.: Elemosina, posola, Eufrosine, proposito, etc.

EXCEPT: *Imposta* (shutter). — *Posta* (office, with deriv. *imposto,* I mail, etc.). —*Apposta* (from *appostare*). (*V.* Rule 1.)
Words ending in *posito,* as *proposito,* etc.

O is CLOSE.

Exceptions:

Boto (*voto*, n. and v.), *botro*, *botte.* — *Dotta* (n. and v.). — *Ghiotta* (n.), *ghiotto*, *gotta.* — *Imbotta*, *inghiotto.*

Ot, Ott.

O is OPEN.

Rule:

When followed by t or tt.

Ex.: Noto, ruota, otto, dotto, ciotola, nottola, etc.

— *Loto, lotta.* — *Nipote.* — *Poto* (v.). — *Otre.* — *Sotto.* — *Voto* (vow., n., and v.).

Derivatives of *ducere* (to lead), as : *condotta, ridotto, prodotto, aquidotto*, etc.

Derivatives of *rompere* and its compounds, as : *rotto, prerotto, corrotto, dirotto*, etc.

Exceptions:

Alcova, altrove. — *Cova, covo* (n. and v.). — *Dove.* — *Giova, giovane, giovo* (giogo). — *Ove.* — *Ricovero* or *ricovro* (n. and v.), *rovere, rovo.* — *Sovero, sovra.*

Ov, Ovv.

Rule:

When followed by v or vv.

Ex.: Piova, ovvio, provvido, manovra, trovo, piovve, etc.

Exceptions:

Gozzo. — *Ingozzo.* — *Mozza, mozzo* (n. meaning waiter; adj. and n. from *mozzare*). — *Pozza, pozzo* (n.). — *Rozzo, rozza* (jade). — *Saragozza, singhiozzo, sozzo.*

Oz, Ozz.

Rule:

When followed by z or zz.

Ex.: Equinozio, ozio, cozzo, bozzolo, Scozia, bozza, etc.

P is pronounced as in English. **Pp** with double emphasis.

Q is always followed by **U,** and pronounced like *qu* in *quart*. Ex.:
Quattro, four.

Qq only occurs in the two words: *Soqquadro,* ruin; *soqquadrare,* to
ruin. It is pronounced with double emphasis.

R is strongly rolled whether it follows or precedes a vowel. Hence
there is no such difference as in the English *bearded, iron,
grain,* etc. Ex.: *Birboneria,* fraud; *ironia,* irony; *grano,* grain.

Rr is rolled with double emphasis, or better, the rolling is pro-
longed. Ex.: *Carro,* wagon; *corro,* I run.

S has two sounds: *hard* and *soft.*

    1. By *hard* sound we mean that of the English **s** in *sea.*
    Ex.: *Se,* if; *casa,* house.

    2. By *soft* sound we mean that of the English **z** in *daze.*
    Ex.: *Caso,* case; *chiesa,* church.

The following tables will enable the student readily to ascertain
whether the **s** is hard or soft.

S is **HARD** (as **s** in **sea**).	**S** is **SOFT** (as **z** in **daze**).
Rule 1:	*Exceptions:*
At the beginning of a word fol- lowed by a vowel or by **c, f, p, q, t.**	*Bisaccia, bisesto. — Esangue. — Filosofo.*

Ex.: Savio, servo, sì, santo, sacerdote, studio, sforzo, etc.

N. B. The same principle obtains when such words are com-
pounded with others.

Ex.: Girasole, dicesi, sconsacrare, risento, etc.

S is **HARD.**	S is **SOFT.**
Rule 2: When it is double. Ex. : Basso, messo, fisso, fosso, etc.	
Rule 3: In adjectives and a number of nouns ending in **osa** and **oso,** and their derivatives. Ex. : Invidioso, glorioso, golosità, maroso, etc.	*Exceptions:* *Tosa* and *toso* (Lombard expression). *Basoso, Esoso.* Words of foreign origin, like : *dose, diocesi, apoteosi, flogosi,* etc.

Rule 4:
In words ending in **esa, ese, esi, eso** (specially in the forms of verbs in *endere*), and their derivatives.
   Ex. : Inteso, compreso, speso, mese, scesi, arnese, arnesino, etc.
	Exceptions :
	Bleso. — Chiesa, cortese, crimenlese. — Francese. — Illeso. —Lesi, leso, Lucchese. — Marchese, Meso. — Obeso. — Paese, palese, and also *palesare* with its different forms.
	   Greek nouns : *Tesi, diaresi, catechesi,* etc.
	   Proper names : *Agnese, Teresa, Creso,* etc.

Rule 5: In the middle of a word when preceded by **l, n, r.** Ex. : Falso, bolso, mensa, borsa, elsa, etc.	

S is HARD.

Rule 6:

When preceded by **ra, re, ri,** at the beginning of a word.
Ex.: Raso (n. and v.), rasojo, riso (n. and forms from ridere), risaja, etc.

S is SOFT.

Exceptions:

Rasente, resina, risico, risipola, and derivatives, *rasentare, resinoso,* etc.

Rule 7:

In compounds and derivatives of the verbs: *ascondere, chiedere, chiudere, porre, ridere, rimanere, rodere.*
Ex.: Ascosi, chiuso, rimase, risposi, risi, la chiusa, il riposo, la posa, etc.

Exceptions:

Clausura, concluso, escluso, recluso, and the like.
Deposito, composito, posizione, sproposito, and the like.
Rosicare, erosione, corrosivo, corrosione, etc.
Derisi, deriso, derisione, irrisione.

Rule 8:

In the following words and their derivatives:
Asino. — Basalte. — Casa, Chiusi, così, cosoffiola. — Desiderio. — Fuso (n.), *fusolo. — Musulmano. — Naso. — Parasito, Pisa, pisello. — Susino, susurro. — Taso.*

S is HARD.	**S is SOFT.**
Exceptions: Words mentioned under Rules 6 and 7.	*Rule 9:* When preceded by a– i– u– and followed by another vowel. Ex.: Asola, basilico, bisogno, fisima, lusinga, fisica, muso, etc.
Exceptions: *Presumere* (not *presuntuoso,* and *presunzione*), *presupporre, Preside, presidente ; presentire, presidio, proseguire, diservire,* etc. (*V.* Rule 1).	*Rule 10:* When the word begins with **esa, ese, esi, eso, esu; osa, ose, oso, osu,** (even though these may be preceded by the consonants **b, c, d, g, l, m, n, p, pr, q, r, s, t**), and their compounds.

Ex.: Esame, esercito, esito, esofago, esusto, Cesare, cesello, desire, mosaico, lesina, prosodia, quesito, rosellina, etc.

Exceptions: Words derived from adjectives in **oso** (*V.* Rule 3), as: *Gelosìa, bramosìa,* etc.	*Rule 11.* When followed by **ia, ie, io.** Ex.: Desio, ambrosiano, etc.
Exceptions: *Cosa, coso. — Posa. — Riposo,* and the other words excluded by Rule 7.	*Rule 12.* When followed by **e** or **o** open. Ex.: Chiesa, doso, elemosina, etc.

S is HARD.	**S is SOFT.**
	Rule 13.
	In the prepositional particles *bis, cis, dis, mis, tras, tris,* in words that begin with a vowel.
	Ex. : Disagio, bisunto, cisalpino, trasandare, misogallo, etc.
	Rule 14.
	When words end in *esimo, esima, osimo.*
	Ex. : Ventesimo, cresima, Cosimo, etc.
Exceptions:	**Rule 15.**
Irrisi, arrisi, sorrisi and derivatives (not *irrisione,* etc.). *V.* Rule 7.	Preterites and Participles in *asi, ase, asero, aso ; isi, ise, isero, iso ; osi, ose, osero, oso ; usi, use, usero, uso ;* and derivative forms (not excluded by Rule 7).
	Ex. : Io misi, ho deriso, diffusamente, persuasivo, etc.

S is HARD.	**S is SOFT.**
	Rule 16.
	In · the following words and their derivatives: *Arrosare — Elemosina — Icosaedro, intisichire — Mausoleo.*

Sc When **sc** precede **e** or **i**, they form a compound consonant with the sound of **sh** in English *ship.* Ex.: *Scena,* scene; *scienza,* science.

Sch is pronounced like **sk** in English *skipper.* Ex.: *Scherzoso,* playful; *schiaffo,* a cuff.

T is pronounced as in English. **Tt** with double emphasis.

U is pronounced like **oo** in *poor.* Ex.: *Puro,* pure.

V is pronounced as in English. **Vv** with double emphasis.

W is pronounced as in the language from which it is borrowed.

X is pronounced as in the language from which it is borrowed.

Y is pronounced as in the language from which it is borrowed.

Z has two sounds: *Hard* and *Soft.*

    1. By *hard sound* we mean that of the English **ts.** Ex.: *Senza,* without.

    2. By *soft sound* we mean that of the English **dz.** Ex.: *Zelo,* zeal.

Zz is sometimes pronounced like **tts,** sometimes like **ddz.**

We append the necessary rules, with a list of exceptions, which it is hoped will be found quite complete.

Rule 1.

Z *is hard* at the beginning of a word.   Ex. : Zana, zecca, zappa, etc.

Exceptions:

zabajone	zanni	zero	zingone	zonzo
zaffe	zanzara	zeugma	zinna	zoofito
zafferano	zara	zeta	zinale	zooforico
zaffetica	zavorra	zezzolo	zirla	zooiatria
zaffiro	zebra	zibaldone	zirlare	zoolito
zaffrone	zeffiro	zibellino	zirlo	zoologia
zagaglia	zelamina	zibetto	ziro	zotico
zaganato	zelo	zibibbo	zizzania	zotomia
zaganella	zendado	ziffe	zizzola	zozza
zaino	zeno	zigolo	zodiaco	zugo
zambecchino	zenit	zigoma	zolla	zurlo
zamberlucco	zenzero	zimarra	zombrare	zurro
zambra	zeolita	zimino	zona	zuzzerullone
zambracca	zerbino	zinco		

And their compounds and derivatives.

Rule 2:

Z is *hard* in the verbal endings *azzare, ezzare, izzare, ozzare, uzzare,* and in all their derivatives.

Ex. : Impazzare, carezzare, rizzare, carezza, puzzo, etc.

Exceptions:

1. Verbs in *izzare* of *more than four* syllables in the infinitive, like : *armonizzare, caratterizzare,* or derived from words *with a*

soft **z**, as: *frizzare, sbuzzare* — or a few that may also be written *with a* **g**. Ex.: *Matrizzare* or *madreggiare; patrizzare* or *padreggiare.*

2. The following verbs: *Abbrezzare, adorezzare, ammezzare* (to half.) — *Battezzare.* — *Dimezzare, dirozzare.* — *Insozzare, intramezzare.* —*Olezzare.* — *Rammezzare, razzare* (from *razzo*), *ruzzare.* — *Sozzare, spetezzare, strabuzzare, suzzare.* — *Tramezzare.*

Rule 3:

Z is *hard* in nouns and adjectives ending in: *azzo, azza ; ezzo, ezza ; izzo, izza ; ozzo, ozza ; uzzo, uzza ;* and when the accent falls on the antepenult; also on those ending in: *azzolo, azzola, azzone,* etc., and their derivatives.

Ex.: Piazza, chiarezza, carrozza, pozzo, pagliuzza, rezzola, etc.

Exceptions:

Amazzone, azzimo (adj. and v.). — *Bazza, bizza, bozzima, brezza, bozza, bozzo* (a pool), *buzzo.* — *Chiozzo.* — *Dosuzza.* — *Frizzo* (n. and v.) — *Gazza* or *gazzera, ghezzo, ghiozzo, ghiribizzo, grezzo.* — *Intirizzo.* — *Lacchezzo, lapislazzuli, lazza, Lazzaro, lazzo* (jest), *lezzo.* — *Mezzo* (half, and its compounds), *mozzo* (nave of a wheel). — *Olezzo, orezzo, ozzimo.* — *Pruzza.* — *Razza* (ray-fish), *razzo* (n. and v.), *rezzo, ribrezzo, rozza* (n.) *rozzo, ruzzo* (n. and v.). — *Sezzo, schiribizzo, sizza, sozzo* (n. and v.) *suzzo* (v. and adj.). — *Uzza, uzzolo.* — *Volezzo.* — *Zizza, zizzola, zozza.*

Rule 4:

Z is *hard* when preceded by another consonant. Ex.: *Forza,* force.

Exceptions:

Abbronzare, alcorza, archipenzolo, arzente, arzica, arzigogolo, arzillo. — Barzelletta, Belzebù, benzina, benzoino, borzacchiare, Bonzo, bronzo. — Calenzuolo, catarzo. — Donzella. — Fronzolo, fronzuto. — Ganza, ganzerino, ganzo, garza, garzo, garzare, garzone, garzuolo, gironzo, gonzo. — Ingarzullito, inzibettato, inzotichire. — Manzo, manzuolo, marzocco. — Orzajuolo, orzeruolo, orza, orzata, orzese, orzo, orzuolo. — Penzolo, pranzare, pranzo. — Ramanzina, rifronzire, rinverzicare, rinverzire, romanzo, ronzare, ronzo (n. and v.), *ronzone. — Sbonzolare, scorza, scorzare, scorzone, sfarzo, sfronzare, sgarza, spenzolo, sverza, sverzare. — Verzicare, verzicolare, verza, verzino, verzotto, verzume, verzura. — Zanzara, zenzevero, zenzero, zonzare, zonzo.*

Rule 5:

Z is *hard* when followed by **io, ia, ie,**   Ex.: Prezioso, etc.

Exceptions:

1. *Azienda, Nazianzo.*

2. Words derived from others with a *soft* z, as : *Romanziere, ronzio, bronziere,* etc.

Zz is *soft* (like **ddz**) in the following unclassified words.

Aguzzino, aggrezzire, allazzerire, arrozzire, azoto, azzeruola, azzeruolo, azzimare, azzimella, azzimina, azzimino, azzollare, azzonare, azzorare, azzuolo, azzurro. — Bazzana, bazzecola, bazzoffia, bazzotto, bizzeffe, buzzurro. — Dozzina. — Gazzarra, gazzella, gazzerio, gazzetta, gazzina, gazzurro, ghiazzerino, ghiazzeruola. — Imbozzacchiare, imbozzimare. — Lazzeretto, lazzerone, lazzeruola, lazzeruolo. — Magazzino, mezzule. — Ossizzacchera, ozena. — Panizzare. — Razzente, razzese, Rezzonico. — Sbizzarrire, sgabuzzino, suzzacchera. — Valezzato.

ACCENTS.

The Tonic Accent.

1. When the Tonic Accent rests upon the last syllable, *l'ultima*, the word is called in Italian *parola tronca*, plur. *parole tronche.*

2. When the Tonic Accent rests upon the penultimate, *la penultima* (this is the case with the *very large majority* of words), the word is called *parola piana.*

3. When the Tonic Accent rests upon the antepenult, *l'antepenultima*, the word is called *parola sdrucciola.*

4. When the Tonic Accent rests upon the syllable before the antepenult, *la quart'ultima*, the word is called *parola bisdrucciola.*

5. The Tonic Accent may go still further back on the *quint'ultima* and the *sest'ultima*, as in *porgamivisene;* but such words are very seldom found.

No absolute rule can be given which will enable one instantly and unhesitatingly to place the Tonic Accent on the proper syllable. Words are generally accented as in Latin ; yet there are a considerable number of rather unjustifiable exceptions.

The Graphic Accent.

Three graphic accents are used : the *Grave*, the *Acute*, and the *Circumflex.*

The **Grave Accent** is used : —

1. On the last vowel of all monosyllables ending in a diphthong, and all other words ending in a vowel, *whenever the tonic accent falls upon it*, whether because of contraction or for any other reason.

Ex. : Già, piè, ciò, può, più, giù ; bontà, credè, venerdì, leggerò, virtù.

2. On a number of monosyllables *to distinguish them* from others otherwise spelled alike.

Ex. : *è*, is, from *e*, and ; *dà*, gives, from *da*, from ; *dì*, day, from *di*, of ; *tè*, tea, from *te*, to thee ; *nè*, neither, from *ne*, of it, etc. ; *nèi*, imperfections, from *nei*, in thee ; *vòi* (vuoi), thou wishest, from *voi*, you ; *dài* (v.), from *dai* (art., prep.).

3. On the last vowel of *shortened forms of the preterite*, to distinguish them from the present infinitive of the same verbs.

Ex. : *amàr* = *amarono*, to distinguish it from *amar* = *amare*.

temèr = *temerono*, to distinguish it from *temer* = *temere*.

nutrìr = *nutrirono*, to distinguish it from *nutrir* = *nutrire*.

N. B. — Some use the circumflex accent in the above cases, claiming thus better to indicate the excision of several letters.

4. While the grave accent is regularly *used on the final syllable only* of words, it may be properly employed also in the following cases :

a. On the **e** or **o** of a penultimate to indicate the *open* sound, in a word which with the close sound would have an entirely different meaning.

Ex. : *òra* = *aura*, zephyr ; *ora*, hour.

b. In certain verbal forms with suffixes, to avoid ambiguity.

Ex. : *dàlle* = *le dà* ; *dalle* = *da le*.

donògli = *gli donò* ; *donogli* = *gli dono*.

amàrti = *ti amarono* ; *amarti* = *amar te*.

c. On the vowel **a** — which has naturally an open sound — on any syllable other than the last, to distinguish homonyms.

Ex.: *dànno*, verb; *danno*, noun; *àbitino*, verb; *abitino*, dim. noun.

N. B. — Some prefer to use the *acute* accent in these cases, as we shall see farther on.

d. On the penultimate vowel of polysyllables ending in two vowels, whenever the tonic accent falls upon it.

Ex.: Giudèo, pazzìa, Menelào, Piròo.

But the majority do not follow this rule except when there may be danger of ambiguity.

Ex.: *balìa*, power; *balia*, nurse; *stropiccìo*, the rubbing; *stropiccio*, I rub.

N. B. — Some use the *acute* accent, but *the grave is preferable.*

The **Acute Accent** is used.

1. And very properly, to distinguish polysyllabic homonyms.

Ex.: *dánno*, verb; *danno*, noun; *séguito* (n. and v.); *seguito*, participle; *ábitino*, verb; *abitino*, noun.

2. Instead of the *Grave* as per Rule 4, d. But, we repeat, the use of the *grave* accent in such cases is preferable.

3. The words *simile, umile, celebre, tenebre, funebre, lugubre, feretro*, and a few others are accented on the antepenult. Poets often use them with accent on the penultimate, and write *simíle, umíle, celébre, funébre, lugúbre, ferétro*, etc. It is better, however, to write *celèbre, tenèbre, funèbre, ferètro*, with the grave accent, thus indicating the open sound of the e.

Some grammarians advocate the use of the *acute* accent on the e of all *parole tronche.*

Ex.: perché, poiché, perdé, credé, etc. But this is not in general use.

Unfortunately, writers and publishers are not unanimous in their adoption of this or that system of accenting. Thus, for instance, in Villari's "Storia di Firenze," Florence, Sansone, 1893, we find the *acute* accent used as follows: *né* (neg.), *a sé, poté, perché, poiché, cosí, s'aprí, seguí, riuscí, piú, virtú*, etc.

The **Circumflex Accent** is used:

1. Upon certain syncopated words, which, if written without accent, might be confounded with others otherwise spelled alike, but having a different meaning.

Ex.: *côrre* = cogliere; *corre*, he runs; *tôrre* = togliere; *torre*, a tower.

2. By some excellent writers and publishers, on the **î**, plural of nouns and adjectives in unaccented **io**, while others use **i, ii, or j**. (*V.* our REMARKS on the use of these in Plural Forms.)

Ex.: studî, municipî, giudizî, feudatarî, necessarî.

NOTE. — When for any reason whatsoever, a graphic accent has to be used on the third or fourth syllable from the last of any word, it is advisable to *use the grave* accent whenever the vowel is to have an *open* sound. This rule is sanctioned by the best writers. Therefore we should write: *càlice, vàlicano, tènere*, etc.

DIVISION OF WORDS INTO SYLLABLES.

1. A consonant between two vowels unites with the following vowel.

Ex.: *a-mo, na-tu-ra, o-do-ro-so.*

EXCEPT in the case of compound words, which are divided in their component parts. Ex.: *dis-onore, ab-uso, mal-agevole, in-esti-mabile.*

2. Double consonants are divided.

Ex.: *an-no, er-rore, bel-lis-simo, spet-tro, sac-chi.*

N. B. — *Apostrophized syllables,* which of themselves contain no sound, should never begin or end a line.

Ex.: Do not write: *d' - oggi, gl' - Inglesi, no -'l so*

But you may write: *que' - tempi ; be' - fiori ; va' - via.*

3. Of two or more consonants, the first unites with the preceding vowel, the other or others with the following.

Ex.: *al-to, con-fon-de-re ; al-tro, den-tro, in-ter-pre-ta-re.*

Exceptions:

a. If **f,** or one of the mutes, **b, c, d, g, p, t, v,** is followed by a liquid (**l, r,** or **n**), both unite with the second vowel.

Ex.: *de-cli-na-re, a-frez-za, co-pri-re.*

b. **S** followed by any consonant or consonants (**s** *impura*) unites with it or them and the following vowel.

Ex.: *o-scu-ro, a-po-sto-lo, mo-stro.*

N. B. *Not,* however, in the case of compound words, as we have seen under Rule I.

Ex.: *legis-latore, tras-gredire.*

c. Compound words in which **c** precedes **q** may be divided in
two ways: by dividing the consonants, or joining them to
the following vowel.

Ex.: *ac-quistare,* or, *a-cquistare.* Moise says that the latter
way is more general.

THE APOSTROPHE.

The ear, better than rules, should guide one in the use of the
apostrophe. For instance, it is quite evident that *l' uso* is more
euphonic than *lo uso.* The following rules, therefore, are more or
less of a general character.

1. The articles or pronouns *lo, la, gli, le* are usually elided when
the next word begins with a vowel.

Gli, however (and all words ending in **gli**), only before **i**.
Therefore we say: *Gl' Italiani, gl' Inglesi;* but *gli Americani.*

2. The pronominal particles *mi, ti, ci, vi, ne, si* are similarly
elided. *Ci,* however, only before **e** or **i**; otherwise its sound would
be hard.

3. The preposition *di* takes the apostrophe before a vowel.

N. B. — The preposition *da* is never elided.

4. The conjunctions *se,* and *che* (and its compounds), are elided.
The latter, preferably, only before **e** and **i**.

N. B. — No monosyllable, other than those mentioned in the
above rules, is ever elided.

5. All words of more than one syllable, ending in a vowel, may
be elided, *unless such a vowel be accented,* in which case the word
must be written in full. The only exceptions are compounds of the

conjunction *che;* such as, *dacchè, giacchè, benchè,* etc., which may take the apostrophe.

6. The apostrophe is also commonly used at the end of words which have dropped a vowel, and some that have lost a syllable.

Ex. : *a'* for *ai; da', dai ; ne', nei ; crede', credei ; sara', sarai ; me', meglio ; mo', modo ; po', poco.*

EXCEPT contracted forms which originally ended in te or de; like, *bontà* (bontade), *mercè* (mercede) ; and the particles *testè, su,* and *giù,* which originally ended in so, but are now considered complete in their modern form.

REMARKS

ON

THE USE OF i, ii, j, í, IN PLURAL FORMS, VERBAL ENDINGS, ETC.

1. **J** (or **î**) is commonly used in the plural of Nouns and Adjectives in *unaccented* **io.**

Ex.: *Esempio, esempj ; principio, principj ; studio, studj ;*
    Socio, socj ; naufragio, naufragj ; rifugio, rifugj.

Exceptions:

a. Nouns ending in *chio, ghio, glio.* As: occhio, mugghio, cespuglio.

b. A few in *cio* and *gio,* in which the **i** is used merely to soften the **c** or **g.** As: arancio, fregio.

These form their plural by changing *io* **into** *i.*

N. B. — Some authorities have advocated, and a number of authors have adopted, the use of **î** instead of *j* to designate the plural of nouns and adjectives in unaccented *io* (excepting those few in *cio* and *gio* mentioned under *b*).

2. As the mark of the plural of Nouns and Adjectives ending in the singular in *jo.*

Ex.: *operajo, operaj ; rasojo, rasoj.*

N. B. — The use of *j* instead of *i* between two vowels is recommended and objected to by equally good authorities, while writers of equal repute differ in their usage.

Ex.: *calamajo, gioja ; muojono ; calamajata, bajonettata,* or *calamaio,* etc.

Use *ii.*

1. In the plural of Nouns and Adjectives ending in *ìo*, with the tonic accent on the *ì*.

Ex. : *natìo, natìi ; calpestìo, calpestìi ; zìo, zìi ; mormorìo, mormorìi.*

2. In verbal endings, such as : *tu odii* (from odiare), *tu allevii* (from alleviare), *tu principii, tu studii, tu incendii, tu varii, tu dubbii, io nutrii, io finii,* etc., to distinguish them from : *tu odi* (from udire), *tu allevi* (from allevare), *principi* (plural of principe), *principj* (plural of principio), etc.

.